MW00513892

Night Writer

Optimize Your Time,
Upgrade Your Skills
and Write Around Your Day Job

Sandee L. Hemphill

Jeremiah One Nine Publishing

Mielle - Congratulations on your Goodreads giveaway win. I look forward to seeing your book when its published.

I wish you continued publishing success.

Sandee Hemphill

Night Writer—Optimize Your Time, Upgrade Your Skills *and* Write Around Your Day Job

Published by Jeremiah One Nine Publishing

Copyright © 2017 by Sandee L. Hemphill

Internet websites and resources referenced may have changed or been removed between the time of publication and the time of purchase of this book.

ISBN 978-0-9828738-4-7
  1. Reference 2. Writing   3. Title: Night Writer

Cover Design: I've Got You Covered

Printed in the United States of America

"

IF THE DESIRE TO WRITE IS NOT
ACCOMPANIED BY ACTUAL WRITING,
THEN THE DESIRE MUST BE NOT TO WRITE."

— *Hugh Prather* —

Introduction

Have you ever wanted to write a book? It's been reported that 72% of Americans have a book in them, but only 14% of them act on it. Some of the reasons for not taking action include fear of rejection; others are the simple fact of working a full-time job, having a family and lots of time-consuming duties. For these people, there is *no time* to write a book.

But here's what they don't know. You *can* carve out time to write and publish a book while working a job. What it takes is a commitment to the task and a solid writing plan, followed by the required action. NIGHT WRITER will walk you through the process of writing around your day job.

Let's be realistic. Writing a book IS NOT an easy task. However, it is an achievable one. It can also be a rewarding activity. It's possible that in only a few months you can participate in a book launch, signing your name to your own publication.

Additionally, your book can launch an expanded career beyond writing. You can launch a speaking career with workshops and keynote speeches. You can further expand your career by creating a workbook to go along with your workshop. In fact, you can create multiple streams of income from your book, depending on how you choose to make use of it. But that's a bit ahead of the program. Let's get the book written first and then we'll use it to cover the earth in other forms.

What you'll learn in NIGHT WRITER will revolutionize your writing. When you apply the tips presented here and make use of the tools we reference, your writing time will shift from boring to soaring. At first, it won't be easy. There will be a host of unscheduled shifts and changes, especially last-minute changes. However, in due time, you'll master these shifts and develop the skills needed to draft your book.

One of the best ways to start a successful writing project is to adopt a write-to-the-finish mindset. A healthy mind will do a lot to produce a healthy outcome. Your mind will be either an asset for you, or an obstacle; you make the choice. You can feed yourself positive self-talk, or you can talk yourself into failing. And you don't want to fail, do you?

Writing is a process. Few, if any, writers can sit down and bang out a book. Writing requires preparation and organization, to say the very least. It also takes a history of successful writings to give you the confidence to move up to larger projects.

Start by writing and publishing a few articles. Group these articles to generate a report. Now you're ready to take on a larger project such as a book. It may not happen to you exactly this way, but this could be a logical progression to your wish to publish a book.

Your writing can go faster if you start with an organized plan. Giving your ideas some direction allows you to move from one section of your writing project to the next. It's great to have your ideas organized in your head, but it's usually better if they're written down. As you'll discover later, there are great benefits to starting your book with an outline.

Some of the writers I work with tell me they can't write from an outline. Some are embarrassed to talk about their writing style because writing with an outline is considered the 'right' way to set up your writing project. What you'll discover later in this book is there is no right or wrong way to set up your book project. What's 'right' is what works for you.

As mentioned before, writing is a skill. Therefore, you can learn to write and improve upon with time and diligence. Let's explore writing in view of a child learning to walk. A child goes through several stages of development before learning to walk. There are (expectedly) several failed missions along the way. But the child never gives up on the idea of walking.

Regardless of how many times the child falls, the day finally comes when the child can stand up and balance themselves, and take a step. They take another, and another, and yet another step. Occasionally they fall, but, of course, they get up and try it again. In fullness of time, there is more walking than there is falling.

This is quite similar to writing a book. You'll fall lots times but you'll also win lots of victories (yeah!).

The main point here is that walking is a progressive act. And so it is with writing a book. You'll write well on some days, and not so well on others. A completed chapter on Monday is tossed in the trash a few days later. Or you'll get near the end of your book and decide a critical chapter is missing. As you see, there will be successes and failures. True success comes when you have more victories than failures.

It's obvious that you're committed to this task (you bought this book) and you're ready to get your book in print. You want to optimize your time, upgrade your skills and write around your day job. That's great! You also understand that as a Night Writer you'll be going against great odds. However, if you prepare yourself properly, you'll enjoy the writing journey.

NIGHT WRITER will prepare you to:
1) Develop a write-to-the-finish mindset
2) Optimize your writing schedule
3) Access the best of today's productivity tools
4) Draft a great book
5) Successfully repeat the process

Let's get started. As a last thought, don't pressure yourself to fit into any artificial writing constraints. Examine all variables before setting goals that will meet your time requirements. Be guided by your own ambition to create a successful book. After all, it's your time, your commitment and your success.

Night Writer
Optimize Your Time, Upgrade Your Skills, *and* Write Around Your Day Job

Contents

1

What's a Night Writer?

NIGHT WRITER isn't a new concept. They've always existed although not necessarily by this name. Some Night Writers see themselves as writers on the sidelines or as part-time writers. However, with the effort required to pen a manuscript, I don't see anything part-time about being a Night Writer.

Yet I know hundreds of writers who are, in fact, sitting on the sidelines and not yet writing. Most of them are waiting for inspiration to come. Or they are stymied by the sheer size of a writing project. Either way, this book is designed to shift them into the drivers' seat and get their book started. And not simply started, but ultimately finished.

There have been hundreds of famous writers who've honed their craft while working a job. Look at this brief list of Night Writers who forged a trail while working around their day job:

Anne Rice *(Interview with the Vampire)* — Worked as an insurance salesperson
Nicholas Sparks *(The Notebook)* — Dental products sales
Toni Morrison *(Beloved)* — Worked as an editor and taught university classes
Douglas Adams *(The Hitchhiker's Guide to the Galaxy)* — Worked as a bodyguard
John Green (The Fault in Our Stars) — Children's hospital chaplain

Night Writer

The term "Night Writer" is applied to anyone who works an 8-hour day and then devotes time to writing. Ideally, they work during the day and write at night. In essence, a Night Writer is a juggler with three balls in the air. They juggle a day job, a writing career and a life (with or without a family).

When it comes to time to write, Night Writers are often challenged by a lack of time and an understandable lack of energy. Enthusiasm wanes from session to session and family life is often compromised. They understand the sacrifices they need to make, but they are committed to this choice. They aren't focused on what they're giving up but on what they'll gain.

There's no question about the difficulty built into the lifestyle of a Night Writer. Trying to give their best to a job and to a writing career and family can be exhausting. Or it can also be equally rewarding. It all depends on the writer's perspective.

"Start where you are, use what you have, do what you can."

— Anonymous

---

7 TOP CHALLENGES OF A NIGHT WRITER (AND HOW TO OVERCOME THEM)

Let's make this perfectly clear. Night Writers face challenges full-time writers can't even dream about. Not only are the best writing hours of the day consumed with making a living, but your body is physically challenged as well. And there's a wind-down period needed to shift gears from employee to writer.

Life doesn't cut you any breaks because you're functioning as a Night Writer. That's why the various tools and resources offered in this book could make a world of difference in your writing. It all depends on your ability to make use of them.

Optimizing your time will help you reach your publishing goals quicker and easier than expected. You'll learn to upgrade your skills and set up limits for future books you write. In essence, you'll create your next success blueprint.

So exactly what challenges do Night Writers face? We'll cover seven of them here.

Challenge #1 — I'm tired.

This is a legitimate complaint. Granted, you've simply given out your best energy of the day. Now you're facing an evening commute, a family waiting to communicate with you, meals to consume, and maybe even a dog to walk. All of this is on your plate and you still want to write a book. Well, it's a lot to do but others have managed this task and so can you.

Solution — Adjust your writing schedule by writing fewer weekdays and doubling up on the weekend. Is it possible to devote two or three lunch hours per week to writing? Can you forego a favorite TV program until your project is at least half-way completed? These are some of the sacrifices a successful Night Writer needs to make.

Challenge #2 — Because I'm already tired, I don't feel sharp enough to write.

You've spent most of your energy on your day job and you want to write a book. Don't allow the tiredness of the day to dictate your evening action. Soldier on!

Solution — It might be easy to give in to this one, but you won't need to. First off, attend to your body's needs by taking a brief nap before your writing time. Have some juice or coffee waiting for you so you are thoroughly refreshed.

As for writing, plan it out during the day. Make a list of opening sentences or map out a full chapter as you get started. When you start to write, you'll know exactly where to begin. You'll forget about being tired and focus on completing the evenings' agenda.

Challenge #3 — I get home late.

It's obvious your full-time job is cutting into your nighttime job (writing). You probably can't change your work hours. But you can manage when, where, and how often you write. Regardless of your work hours, you can still get in some writing time.

Solution —If you're getting home late, you may want to shift your schedule to write *before* you go to work. And don't try to write for an hour or two; try 20-25 minutes of dedicated writing before going to work (see the *Pomodoro Technique* in Chapter 4). Be prepared to take advantage of the unexpected breaks in your day. You'll find other suggestions in *Appendix A—Productivity Tools*.

Challenge #4 — When I get home my wife wants me to spend time with her and the family.

This is a reasonable request. If your wife is supporting your writing career, she'll still want a stable home environment. There are lots of activities you'll need to sacrifice to be a Night Writer, but your family time is not recommended.

Solution — Have a family meeting and explain to everyone the goal you're trying to reach. Then share your proposed writing schedule. This should include time for family dynamics and time to write. Stress the fact that on your writing days, you need to dedicate yourself to that assignment. Of course, there'll be times when last-minute adjustments will need to be made. But by being flexible with your schedule, you'll have time to write and build even stronger family bonds.

Challenge #5 — There's always a crowd in my house; I can't find a quiet place to write.

This isn't a unique situation; hundreds of Night Writers face this same problem. You may have lots of rooms in your house but may also have lots of people crammed in them. How do you fulfill your writing schedule under these circumstances?

Solution — Find a room that is the farthest away from your family. Set up your writing station and get to work. Make this a regular location even if the house isn't crowded. One of my clients was on a strict deadline and a set up a makeshift office in her walk-in closet. She added a small desk with a clip-on lamp for extra lighting. Her makeshift office helped save the day. She met the deadline with time to spare.

Challenge #6 — My work and writing schedule doesn't leave much time to do extra activities.

Finding time to do what we love to do is an ongoing challenge. When you are a Night Writer, bear in mind that it's only for a designated time. Life will go on after you write your book.

Solution — All work and no play makes ... you know the rest of this saying. Build time in your schedule to play. If you are longing for certain activities, adjust your book deadline in order to participate, especially if it is an annual event. Otherwise, you'll want to stay focused and work on your book. Then you'll have lots of time for these activities.

Challenge #7 — Sitting alone at my keyboard makes me want to eat.
Trying to write while thinking of food is bound to be a problem. Could it be you'd rather be with the family eating popcorn and watching a movie instead of sitting by yourself and writing?

Solution — Focusing on your evening's assignment is a must for completing your book. Eating and writing are not recommended at the same time. At least not eating a full meal while writing. The breaks in your thought pattern would be a distraction to your writing task.

Try to eat an hour before you begin your writing session. You can also keep water, juice and nuts near your workstation to support you when hunger strikes. Also, frequent breaks will refresh you and hopefully take your mind off eating.

Challenge Summation: Don't let the daily grind rob you of the energy you'll need later in the day. Learn how to optimize the time you have so you can shift your writing into overdrive.

This can also be accomplished by upgrading your skills.

Remember, your primary goal is to write, and to write well on a regular schedule. This builds your writing stamina. The more stamina you bring to your writing time, the sooner you can finish the day's schedule. This will also pay off big in the total time it takes to complete the book.

BALANCING ACT

There are lots of activities a Night Writer can't engage in; then again, there are lots they can. It all begins with balance. Of course, balance can mean different things to different writers. However, once you define what balance is for you, you'll have to fight to keep it.

Generally, Night Writers maintain balance by incorporating these writing rituals:
- Write as regularly as possible
- Schedule writing time, then make it sacred (this means make your family and friends respect it)
- Listen to other writers' advice but only if they're successful
- If what you're writing doesn't excite you, you don't want to write it (yes, writing is a chore but it shouldn't be a bore. If it doesn't excite you, it probably won't excite the reader.)

Consider these pointers for maintaining a balance between writing and working:
- Build your writing career book by book (don't wait for a big hit to arrive)
- For efficiency, duplicate the time management system you apply on your day job to your Night Writer schedule
- Identify and remove any time wasters from your writing routine, but remember the benefits of regular breaks
- Writing a page a day may not be much content, but it's still brings you a page closer to the last chapter of your book

- Keep a writing productivity app on hand to take advantage of open time slots
- Increase productivity by using the tools, tips and the apps given in *Appendix A—Productivity Tools* (you'll find lots of them listed there).
- Don't forget to schedule some time to play

Not everyone is skilled at striking a balance between being a day worker and a Night Writer. Regardless of your passion, it will take time and patience to get this lifestyle to a workable level. Be patient with yourself and the writing process.

DEVELOP A WRITE-TO-THE-FINISH MINDSET

Believe it or not, writers (full-time writers and Night Writers) often abandon their writing projects. Time is a key factor for a bailout. For some writers, the demands are much more than expected. Others tire out long before the mid-point. But on the other hand, it's also possible the writer did not adequately prepare for the mental requirements of the writing journey. Half-hearted preparation coupled with a lack of commitment to a writing schedule will always derail a book's completion.

Your plan is to be a successful writer (again, you bought this book so I think this is a fair assumption). Therefore, you'll need to bring a write-to-the-finish mindset to your writing project. This means you must be tenacious in your approach to writing your book. You should envision the book in your hand and continue to move forward toward the finish line.

Here are five ways you can adopt and execute a write-to-the-finish mindset and experience writing success:

Develop patience
Night Writers are challenged more than other writers (full-time, freelance, etc.). Therefore, you'll need to learn patience. Unfortunately, patience is not a lesson you learn only once. It

will probably be repeated again. Remember you are on a journey. Allow yourself the time needed to complete it.

Walk before you run

There is no reason for you to bring underdeveloped skills to your project. Take a writing class (online or in person) before you start writing your book. Update your grammar; learn a new software or master an app that can offer you a time savings privilege. Yes, this may put your project off a bit, but it would be better to finish well than to finish poorly.

Learn how to eat an elephant

You know the riddle about eating an elephant, right? You eat him one bite at a time. Learn to apply this logic to your book project and break up your tasks into bite-size pieces.

If you plan to write a chapter each evening, quickly mind-map where you think you want to go during your writing session. This gives a new perspective to the task and will help you get to the end of your writing session much faster.

Set boundaries

You cannot produce quality work if you are constantly reacting to other people's issues. There are limits on your creative time. The time you have is precious and requires your undivided attention. You must learn to guard your writing time so you can maximize your productivity. Try to avoid the people and situations that rob you of your creative energy.

Focus, Focus, Focus!

Did I say focus? A Night Writer can easily be distracted. But you can get ahead of the game by setting your eye on the prize. Don't isolate your tasks; look at the big picture. How does tonight's writing session relate to the entire book-writing project? How much closer to the finish line will you be when you complete all of the week's assignments? By looking forward, you can stay excited about the process you make.

When you're focused on your writing goals there are fewer chances of you getting off track. Sure, it takes a lot to stay focused, but if this was easy, everyone would be doing it. Keep your goals in mind and you'll find it easier to stay focused.

WRAPPING UP

As a Night Writer, you're in a unique league of writers. You'll face lots of challenges and perhaps more than a few setbacks. Your key to success will be preparedness.

When you apply the many tips we've provided in this chapter, you can expect to have a much more enjoyable writing journey. It may be a slow for a while, but in due time you'll pick up speed. Before you know it you'll have enough books under your belt to constitute a sizeable writing career, even if you only write part-time.

Learn to honor what you can do with the circumstances you have. Affirm your "Write-to-the-Finish" mindset to keep you motivated. And by all means, work at a pace that works best for you.

Consider the tips we've provided as suggestions rather than rules. That being said, feel free to break them as needed. The truth is, you'll need to customize them to meet your specific needs. Most will only take a small bit of tweaking to get them to your liking. Explore using them in different scenarios and at differ times in your books' development.

Don't shoot yourself in the foot by comparing yourself to what other writers are producing. A better comparison would be to compare yourself with the writer you were last week, or the writer you were six months ago. If you make yourself your own competition, you'll always come out on top.

2

Debunking Negative Self-Talk and Working/Writing Myths

This chapter focuses on one of the issues that deter most would-be writers from taking the plunge. They talk themselves out of writing a book before they get to the first sentence. Many get bogged down with a bad case of the "what ifs'..." such as:

- "What if I'm not qualified to write?"
- "What if I can't write a decent sentence?"
- "What if no one likes my story?"
- "What if I get started but can't finish the book?"
- "What if I finish the book but can't sell it?"

These "what if's" serve as the background of your negative self-talk. But you can reverse these thoughts.

With a bit of preparation, you can easily remove these hurdles.

Knowledge is a solid cure for negative self-talk. You can also cover some ground by upgrading your writing skills. By learning how to write better you'll position yourself for writing success. Learning how to properly structure your book is a skill every writer needs. All of these skills require some self-examination, but it's a painless process. The sooner you give hese issues some attention, the more prepared you'll be for success.

REVERSING YOUR NEGATIVE SELF-TALK

I'm not qualified to write a book.

Says who? You're as qualified as you think you are. All you need to write a book is to garner up some passion and take action. Passion may occasionally wane but as long as you are taking some type of forward action, you'll move the process along. Regardless of your education, career and life's experiences, people will find your book exciting and want to read it.

I'm not a good writer and my grammar isn't current.

You may not begin your writing career as a "good" writer, but you will hone your skills as you continue to write. What's more important is that you can pen a book that readers will want. Additionally, a good editor can upgrade content you may consider mediocre and make it literally sing.

If you're a bit rusty with your grammar, take heart. Its not an impossible challenge and one you can remedy in only a few weeks. There are hundreds of online writing courses you can attend to upgrade your skills. You can check within your local community for writer's groups and courses they might offer.

My story stinks.

A writer is always his own worst critic. Your story may stink to you, but what does your reading audience think? Jump into communities like Goodreads (https://www.goodreads.com) and Wattpad (https://www.wattpad.com) and post chapters of your book to see what others may think. Be sure to target your specific audience. When possible, blend their suggestions into yours and keep moving forward.

I've run out of ideas. I'm quitting!

This is a common sentiment of Night Writers. This is where your prep time comes in to save the day. If you are using an outline or book template, you'll know exactly what step to take next. This preparation will keep you from running out of ideas and help build your excitement about writing.

If you are a creative and write freely, a few tips will keep you going. Skip ahead to another chapter and come back to the first one later. Simply highlight the place you're stopping to help you find your place when you return. By moving ahead to another chapter, you'll jumpstart thoughts for the first one.

Regarding quitting, if I had a dollar for every time I quit a book project, I wouldn't be writing this one. Every one gets frustrated and discouraged during the writing journey. This simply means your not-so-good days have outnumbered your good ones. But hang in there—the good ones will resurface.

In the meantime, it's a good idea to walk away from the entire project for a day or two. This will birth a fresh perspective to add to your story.

I don't know how to sell my book.
Don't get overly concerned about this one. No one knows how to sell a book, at least not at first. In time you'll discover lots of ways to get your book into the hands of your targeted reader.

Ideally, you'll begin a promotional campaign as you're writing the book. Check my website for ideas and resources on this topic, www.workyourbook.com.

"Your goal as a writer should be to maximize your output. Only by producing more writing will you ultimately produce better writing."

— Tom Corson-Knowles

DEBUNKING WRITING/WORKING MYTHS

If you ask around your workplace I'm sure you'll find two or three people who hoped to write a book. But for them, the workday is a barrier to writing success. I'm sure they still have the task on their bucket list, and are probably wondering if it's one they'll ever complete. Don't tell them I said this but more than likely, they won't even begin.

This isn't a problem for you because it's obvious you've already begun. In this section we'll bust seven myths in regard to writing a book while working a full-time job. Let's begin.

MYTH #1 — My day job eats up my writing time.
   Myth-Buster: It's possible to work and write but it requires careful planning, dedication, and time optimization. It's not enough to create a writing schedule; you must also be committed to maintaining it.

Take a look at where some former Night Writers worked before they become famous:
   • Stephen King was a janitor who threw out his first draft of *Carrie*
   • Harper Lee was an airline reservationist before she penned *To Kill a Mockingbird*
   • John Green, the writer of *The Fault in Our Stars,* was inspired by stories of people he met when he worked as a chaplain at a children's hospital
   • *The Notebook* was written by Nicholas Sparks, who sold dental products over the phone before he published his book and met with a measure of success

As you can see, there are lots of Night Writers who joined the writing/working corps. At least you're in good company.

Regardless of your workday schedule, becoming a successful writer is all in the planning. For example, you can:
   • Write during your lunch period
   • Write on the train on your way to and from work
   • Schedule some time during the weekend to write
   • Occasionally opt out of a family activity to dedicate time to writing

- Record hot ideas on your phone or tablet
- Get up earlier (45-90 minutes) to jumpstart your day
- Take a day's vacation to write (maybe away from home)
- Rotate between writing mornings and evenings

These are the types of adjustments you'll need to consider to complete your writing. If you take writing seriously, you'll find time to dedicate to it.

MYTH #2 — You're not an expert.

Myth-Buster: Not every writer starts out as an expert. However, publishing a book adds to your credibility. Besides, you don't need to be an expert to write a book. What you need is knowledge on a specific topic paired with a unique perspective. There you have it—write a book and become an expert.

MYTH #3 — You may be able to write a book, but you can't write a best-selling book while working a full-time job.

Myth-Buster: Here's proof of a writer who worked full-time and penned a best seller. In fact, I'm not sure how Anne Rice had time to write as she held various jobs. She also worked as a waitress, cook and theater usher. Anne worked as an insurance claim examiner while writing, "*Interview With The Vampire.*"

MYTH #4 — You can't work full-time and commit to a writing schedule.

Myth-Buster: This is a big misconception. I think what people mean is you can't have the same writing schedule week after week. This is true for some writers. Having a daily routine of the same time every day can be a boost to your writing project. It can also be unrealistic. A chat with several well-known and not-so-well-known writers found the idea of a regular schedule a laughing matter. Most thought what you really need is a flexible schedule that gets the results you need.

Let's say that on Monday your writing time is 6:30-8:00 am. On Tuesday you write from 4:30-6:30 pm. You skip writing on all on Wednesdays or Thursdays. Friday's schedule includes writing during lunch (while at work) followed by writing at home 7:30 to 10 pm.

Saturday's schedule consists of editing research, if needed. You should take Sunday off so you can start fresh on Monday.

Yes, this is a very flexible schedule, but one which meets your needs. And if you need to make adjustments to this schedule (as any writer would), you can do so without any sense of guilt or project delay.

MYTH #5 — Writers work only when inspiration strikes them.

Myth-Buster: You cannot afford to sit around and wait for inspiration. Inspiration cannot be scheduled. However, it will show up if you do. You should begin writing and expect the inspiration to surface. One way to provoke inspiration is to start writing on a favorite chapter or on a challenging character. Or you can go back to the last writing assignment and review it (to refresh yourself, not to edit). If this doesn't help, swap shifts. Make this an editing day instead of a writing day. Be sure to revise your schedule to reflect the swap. Stay on track by making your next editing day a writing day.

MYTH #6 — Working kills your writing inspiration.

Myth-Buster: This isn't true, or it least it doesn't have to be true. Your job could, in fact, be your main source of inspiration. Many writers pen what they know and live on their jobs. Attorneys pen books about the law and they often include attorneys in their stories. The same is true for doctors and other professionals.

Author John Green was mentioned before in this book. He wrote *The Fault in Our Stars*. He was on track to become an Episcopal priest. Instead, while working with children suffering from life-threatening illnesses, he used their stories to pen his best selling book. How's that for workplace inspiration!

MYTH #7 — Writing takes a lot of time.

Myth-Buster: Writing can take up a lot of time, but it doesn't have to be this way. Procrastination is the enemy of any task. Unless you learn to optimize your time, you'll surely fall prey to Parkinson's Law. This law says, *"Work expands to fill up the time allotted to it."* This easily applies to writing. If you allow it, writing will take a lot of time. You'll get a better handle on your project if you execute a writing plan.

Under Parkinson's Law, you'll find that your chapters or book deadlines continue to expand due to the time you've allotted to your writing project. If you start your writing session without any preparation, you could waste half of your session.

You can easily reverse this law by executing the Pomodoro Technique, a writing formula that uses a timer to help you focus and write faster. You'll learn about this strategy in *Chapter 4 — It's Not Your Time; It's Your Skill.*

WRAPPING UP

Writing myths are a dime a dozen. We only covered a few of them here. You'll find them quite discouraging if embraced. Don't buy into them.

Work to keep your mind on your goals. The bottom line is your writing project will be what you bring to it. Therefore, learn as much about the writing process as you can and execute what you learn.

There are readers waiting for a fresh perspective on your topic. You don't want to delay their satisfaction any longer than necessary.

3

Plan or Plunge:
The Outline Dilema

Should I Use an Outline Or Not Use an Outline to Write My Book? Among authors, this is a really big question. There have been countless debates about using outlines. It's a very personal matter among writers. The determining factor is the method that increases your productivity the most.

Traditionally, non-fiction writers use an outline to draft their books. They view outlines as blueprints to move them step-by-step to the finished product. Having an outline makes it easy to define the problem and envision the solutions you'll want to present in a non-fiction book.

On the other hand, fiction books are imaginative. They might include unlimited plots, twists and storylines. They develop their own characters and scenarios.

A large number of fiction writers believe an outline is a mental straight jacket. They believe it restricts the flow of creativity and blocks new ideas. For these writers, an outline leads to a rigid expression of their content rather than an organic flow (which is sometimes interpreted as *artistic*). They prefer to let their narrative forces guide them rather than an outline.

The truth is, there are no cookie cutter writers. Therefore, there are no right or wrong decisions about using an outline. There is only selection. Match a method (outline or no outline) with your writing skills and your personality to determine a preference. This offers the best expression of the real you through your writing.

---

*"You don't need more time in your day.
You need to decide."*

— Seth Godin

The PLAN Method: WHY YOU (MAY) WANT AN OUTLINE

Give these questions your undivided attention: Can you describe the main theme of your book in a single sentence? Can you describe it in two sentences? You shouldn't have any trouble answering these simple questions.

Here's another question to consider. Would a contractor erect a building without a blueprint? Of course he wouldn't. So why would you attempt to write a book without an outline. An outline (PLAN) is your writing blueprint. A detailed book-writing outline should include these features:
- Help you easily retain your focus
- Increase productivity by writing in chunks
- Help deter writers' block
- Eliminate the dreaded "blank page" syndrome
- Keeps your book from expanding and becoming unmanageable
- Provides guidance and motivation
- May help you focus your marketing efforts
- Can help you format an "elevator speech" for your book
- Visually presents the scope of your book without having to read every word
- You may get to the end of the book faster with this method

As noted, there are various benefits to creating a book outline, but only if this is the way you are most comfortable in penning your story. Of course, there are other ways to outline a book that may prove productive but aren't listed in this book. Also, there is the no-outline method known as the PLUNGE. We'll discuss this method later in this chapter.

HOW TO OUTLINE A BOOK

My search on this topic produced more than 15 ways to outline a book. I'll share only a few of them here to avoid overwhelm.

The basic book outline method involves writing out your title followed by chapter headings and sub-headings. You can write long hand, or use Word or PowerPoint. You can use Evernote or Excel. You can express this method more visually by using sticky notes or index cards. Any one of these tactics will give you the desired result: a usable book outline.

The Skeletal Method
This method of outlining a book gives you a big picture outline of the overall flow of your story. Try this simple seven-step strategy for outlining a fiction book (as presented by Samuel Loveland*)
- Hook
  - Plot Step 1
  - Pinch
- Midpoint
  - Plot Step 2
  - Pinch
- Resolution

*http://samuelloveland.com/writing/story-skeleton-a-simple-seven-step-outline/

Chapter-by-Chapter Method
This is a way to organize the facts of your book and blend them with those of the prior chapter and the next chapter to follow:

- Start with the title of your book
- Now write out your chapter headings (add a few words to each heading to keep the storyline visible)
- Add subheadings to each chapter (again, add a few words to keep the storyline visible)
- Examine your finished outline and make adjustments
- Set your outline aside for at least 24 hours
- Return to your outline and make adjustments if needed

Writing Software
Most of these offer ease of use, advance editing and more.
- SmartEdit
- Scrievener
- WriteItNow
- After the Deadline
- AutoCrit

The Snowflake Method
- Created by fiction author Randy Ingermanson who believes "Good fiction doesn't just happen. It's designed."
- Basic premise is to start small then expand
- Start with one line, add a paragraph, then add a chapter
- See *References* for a detailed look at this method

The Reverse Outline
- Looks at the story from a different perspective
- Start with the ending
- Outline backwards to get to the start

PLUNGE: WRITING WITHOUT AN OUTLINE

Most of the writers I know who write without an outline are fiction writers. They function on the creative writer spectrum. These no-outline writers believe less planning time gives them more writing time. Or at least this is their interpretation of the topic.

These writers tend to view an outline as a straight jacket for their creativity. They wouldn't consider using an outline. Quite often they tell me they can see the story's ending without needing to write out the path the story takes. Kudos if this method works for you.

PLUNGE writers tend to wing it. They can produce a chapter or two of their book with absolutely no pre-planning or any forethought. They don't need written plots or outlines to get their creative juices flowing. According to their accounts, when they sit down the content flows.

Many of them have no habits or rituals that prompt a writing session. Some have no scheduled times to write or any favorite writing places. Some even reject the tools designed to make the writing task easier. They live in their own writing world and make up any rules they need as they write.

The no-outline diehards believe that writing should be the art of creating. They believe you get to what needs to happen as you write. This far exceeds the task of completing a pre-set outline for the day. No outline means fresh, organic prose.

Some fiction writers make use of the available tools to sharpen their skills and produce a faster product. They find it necessary to plot out the first three or four chapters of a book to get started. They have writing schedules and rituals such as eat first, then write. Some crave caffeine before they even consider touching a keyboard. Personally, I prefer a cup of no-caffeine Rooibos tea to start my day. What's your morning ritual?

NO PLAN, NO PROBLEM!

Are you taking the PLUNGE? No problem. It's all in how you approach your story. Bear in mind that what works for one writer may not work for another. You'll have to determine which method works best for you and your topic. You may use both methods at different times in your project.

Consider the following no-outline scenarios:

Shift Beyond Three Acts
- Showcase your characters in a dramatic way
- Show the relationship between tension, conflict, escalation of tension, loss, climatic encounters and unexpected ending
- Develop transformation within a character or a situation

Tension-Filled Background
- Your story will need believability, constant escalation, some casualties, exploding scenes, setbacks, surprises, continuity (pace, speed), genre and fulfilling of expectations
- Build tension by using voice, mood, setting, raising the stakes, dynamic engagement, or ongoing give-and-take

Questions With No Wrong Answers
- Start with the basic idea of your story
- Ask questions until your idea makes sense to you such as:
    — What do your characters care about?
    — What major obstacles will you overcome?
- Your story should easily answer these questions
- Let each answer guide you to the next question
- You're done when you have no more questions

THE FINAL RESOLUTION

Well, the conflict of our outlining issue (pun intended) is this: do you write with or without an outline? You'll need to decide which method works best for your writing style.

You could combine strategies to get the outcome you desire. Consider using one method for a part of your book, and use another method for the other part.

Beyond the outline question, these questions may be asked more frequently in order to increase your writer efficiency and your productivity:

- What do you absolutely, positively need to keep your writing authentic?
- Does outlining your story inhibit your creative flow?
- Can you use an outline to jumpstart your thoughts but not be restricted by it?
- Does writing freestyle keep you focused on a blank canvas without any boundaries?

Only you can decide which method is best for you.

WRAPPING UP

So what's the verdict? Will you PLAN or PLUNGE? It's all up to you which method (or methods) you elect. Your readers don't care if you use the PLAN or the PLUNGE method. What really matters to them is the outcome.

The goal or providing this content is to help you review what's available. It's your option alone to select the method that results in your book being completed in the fastest and easiest way possible. Therefore, the specific method you choose should fit into your writing habits and your lifestyle.

It's possible to incorporate both PLAN and PLUNGE in writing your book. There are not rules to say it should be one of the other. It's all a matter of what you feel comfortable with on any given day. If you can wed the two, more power to you!

By the way, regardless of which method you select (PLAN or PLUNGE), you should always set a deadline for completing your book. This removes the abstract finish line and should help you stay on the task. Otherwise, you'll be writing forever with no end in sight. As a rule, you may want to add an additional month or two to the date to account for legitimate interruptions and unforeseen delays.

4

It's Not Your Time; It's Your Skill

120 wpm. This was once my highest typing speed. It probably doesn't mean anything now, not with computers and all. But this was on an IBM typewriter (do you even remember IBM?). It was a big deal back in the day.

Is this important today? Does your keyboard speed have anything to do with your ability to get a book completed? Let's say "Yes" for now. It's not that speed doesn't matter but it's more important to have upgraded writing skills.

"Writing is easy.
All you have to do is cross out the wrong words."
— Mark Twain

There is still much we can say about keyboard speed. But for today's writer, speed gives way to skill. Skill is what you'll need to write and finish your book.

There are lots of skills you can develop to gain a favorable writer status (language, research, generate fresh ideas, etc.). We'll explore a few tips and tools to determine how to optimize them for your book. If you've already developed the skills we list here, perhaps you can upgrade them. If not, you can learn them. Either way you'll have an updated list of resources to make use of in the future.

WRITE BETTER, WRITE FASTER

Honing your writing skills will serve to help you produce more content in less time. Use the following tips to further develop your writing skills:

Jumpstart Your Writing Juices
Start with your favorite chapter or character. This will launch your creative juices and help you start the creative flow.

Ask Questions
If your writing juices stop flowing, ask questions about the previous content and answer it in the next paragraph.

Begin With the Ending
Start writing on the last chapter of the book and work toward the first chapter. This reserve order does much to activate your writing flow.

Write in Chunks
Block out several hours of the day or a half-day and dedicate it to writing. If you get stuck on a certain chapter simply move to another one. Schedule breaks between chunks of writing.

Get Techy
Today's tech tools are a game-changer for any writer. Become proficient in several easy-to-learn and easy-to-use programs to complete more writing with less effort:
- Writing software: Smart Edit, Scrivener, or Write It Now
- Text editors: After the Deadline, AutoCrit or Grammarly
- Apps (Hemingway, Phraseology or Omniwriter)

(Note: see *Appendix A—Productivity Tools* for details on these and other tools).

Writing is a Learned Skill

Remember that writing is a learned skill. This means you can upgrade it. Seek out writing courses and look for workshops to improve your writing skills. Start with baby steps and improve as you move forward.

Ready, Set, Capture.

You can capture impulsive, creative ideas by having a recording system at your fingertips at all times (consider using tools such as Notes, Evernote, recording apps or devices, etc.).

Map It Out

Organize your ideas before you begin your writing session. You can quickly jot down the path you plan to take. If your writing slows up, check your notes and keep moving.

Write Today, Edit Tomorrow

Set specific days to write and other days to edit; don't do them both on the same day. By keeping these tasks separate, you'll limit the interruptions to the writing or editing flow. This way you'll optimize the time dedicated to either task.

Make Use of Timesavers

Learn to use MultiMarkdown (MMD), a short-cut tool created by Fletcher T. Penney to turn minimally marked-up plain text into well formatted documents for your readers (see *Appendix A—Productivity Tools*)

Measure Writing by Time, Not Words

This is a bit tricky because we talk about books in terms of word count. Use word count to measure the total page count of your book. When writing, measure productivity in terms of time (minutes and hours) and frequency (number of sessions you write per week) instead of measuring by your word count.

Voice Your Book

If your thoughts come faster than you can write them down, use a dictation program to speak it out and transfer it to your writing program. Most smartphones and tablets have a recording app. You'll want a program that allows you to download your content into a writing program (or at least rich text).

You can purchase a small, hand-held recorder to use if it meets your needs. Before completing your purchase, check the final output formats and directions.

MASTER THE POMODORO TECHNIQUE

You'll find this resource is referenced in *Appendix A—Productivity Tools*. However, it's such an important tool it warrants being covered here in detail.

The Pomodoro Technique is an ideal platform for writers to:
- Quickly draft a book
- Motivate yourself to write
- Limit distractions
- Keep track of how long you're spending brainstorming vs. writing vs. revising
- Reduce body tension by moving around during breaks

Here's how the Pomodoro Technique works:
- Select a task (start a new chapter; develop an outline)
- Set a timer for 25 minutes (physical or digital timer)
- Make an oath with yourself that you'll work on the assigned task—and nothing else—for 25 minutes
- When the timer rings, stop working
- Take a break (5-10 minutes)
- Start a new task or complete the first one by resetting the timer for another 25 minutes
- If you complete four sessions in a row, take a longer break (20-30 minutes)
- If you complete eight sessions you'll produce four hours of focused work; make your break a half-hour long
- Reward yourself for finishing all of your day's sessions

The Pomodoro Technique is not rocket science. Some writers

laud this method while others find it pointless. But if you need a quick and easy tool to help you stay focused on writing, why not give it a try?

When I used it, I was literally amazed at the focus and clarity this simple system provided. One of the features I enjoyed about this technique is there was no program to open or app to download. Simply set a timer and get busy.

DEVELOP REUSABLE SYSTEMS

As writers, there are some features of writing that are repeated over and over again. Take, for example, your basic outline. It should alternate only slightly from book to book. If you copy and save a blank book outline, you then have a template to use for future books. This creates an upgrade to your resources.

You can do the same with your book chapters. You can create a chapter template to save you time and effort. Here's an example. The format for this book is one of my basic templates. It includes a simple call-out format.

Variety in formatting the book is achieved by applying different chapter templates. I also have a variety of call-out templates that create a different look. One of these designs, the oversized quote, is used in this book to generate more interest and help the quote stand out even more.

This is what one of my templates dictates for my solo quotes (this is a quote that has nothing else on the page):
- Open quote is 36 pt. font, Times New Roman, color is dark grey, centered
- Quote text is Arial 14 pt. font, all caps, centered
- Author's name is Sign Painter font, 18 pt., with an em dash (−) on both ends

- Closing quote (at the end of the quote) is the same size, font, and same color as the general quote text
- There is a 4 pt. space between the quote and the authors' name
-

Here's another template example taken from this book:

- Quotes are centered within two lines that extend the full width of the page; lines are Georgia font, 8 pt. using underscore character
- Quotes are Georgia font, 12 pt., italic, flanked by open and closing quotes
- Author's name is centered, Arial font, 12 pt., with an em dash (—) before and after the authors' name

Can you see how simple this is? This can be a game changer. I have four or five designs saved and can alternate them as desired. Likewise, I have several book outline templates at the ready. The book outlines and chapter templates are flexible and can easily be mixed and matched to create new book layouts at will. This keeps the book layouts fresh and inviting.

When time permits, set up a host of book and chapter templates. You can do the same for appendices and other features of your book.

EDIT BETTER, EDIT FASTER

Self-editing is a must for any writer. However, it's only one of many edits you will perform on your book. The more errors you catch through the self-edit, the better off you'll be for the last edit.

What this could mean is your last edit will take less time to complete, subtracting days from your timeline. This could also mean a great deal in savings when you get a professional edit.

Self-editing is challenging process. Most writers see what they meant to write rather than what they actually wrote. This is the main reason you don't a self-edit to be the book's final edit. Also, bear in mind that your first edit will most likely result in more of a rewrite than correction.

Use the tips below to prep your book for a great edit.

Go Fishing
Before you begin, allow yourself a few days separation between completing the last draft and starting the first edit. Staying away from the writing environment for a brief time will do you

lots of good. You'll begin the edit phase refreshed, renewed and excited about taking on this challenging task.

Edit Out Loud

Train your ear to hear what you've written by reading your content out loud. Start by editing your book on the computer. Resize the page (zoom) as large as you find comfortable. Now read through the content. When you find something questionable, simply highlight it and return to correct it later.

To, Too, Two
All writers fall prey to some troubling words. Check out this resource to help you identify and correct repetitive words. Get a copy of the most recent copy of *Grammar Girl's Quick and Dirty Tips for Better Writing*, available at Amazon and here: *http://www.quickanddirtytips.com/grammar-girl.*

Read to a Crowd
Read your book to an audience of three to five people to expand on the "*Edit Out Loud*" tip. Having another set of ears is bound to work in your favor. They could catch some issues you hadn't noticed before. And gathering feedback from an unbiased audience could do much to take your book to the next level.

Beyond Spellcheck

Did you know that MS Word's spellcheck program has only a 30% accuracy rate? Even though spellcheck knows the difference between "its" and "it's," it often makes the wrong recommendation. Granted, no serious writer would depend on spellcheck alone, but you'll be surprised at how many truly do. I'd suggest you find an online editing app for the self-edit phase of

your book (see *Appendix A—Productivity Tools)*.

Eliminate Your Top 10

Do you know what your top 10 repeated words or phrases are? If so, then you probably know you are overusing them. Several of the software programs we list in *Appendix A—Productivity Tools* will help you search out your most frequently used words. Otherwise, check for them yourself when you read out loud as an edit strategy.

Friends with Degrees

Who doesn't have a friend with a degree or two? Unless your friend has a degree in English or some experience as a professional editor they DO NOT qualify as editors.

An editor is one who will make your book more credible for the intended audience. This is an important part of book preparation. It requires a fine eye and attention to detail. Don't hand over editing to friends who lack proper credentials. Keep your friendship intact and find a professional editor.

Third Time's a Charm

Schedule three edits of your book. You can do the first edit if you follow the suggestions we've made. You'll want to dig into the book's foundation and conduct a line-by-line search for spelling and grammar errors. The second edit should be conducted by an editing professional. This is when you'll rewrite chapters or scenes. They'll also conduct the last edit, which prepares you to go to the publisher.

SILENCE YOUR INNER CRITIC

You want to publish a book. You want the world to read it and learn your heart on a certain topic. Yet you often find a little voice telling you what you can't do with regard to writing your book. It's your inner critic: it's the endless voice in your head telling you something is wrong.

If you give in to these thoughts, you create a break in your writing focus.

Your inner critic slows down your writing by shifting your focus from your impending success to failure. You must learn to turn off the critic. Yes, this is easy to say but hard to do. You must learn to silence these voices or you'll never complete your writing task.

Here are some ways you can reject and even remove these self-defeating voices:
- Join a writing group so others are regularly critiquing your work and offering positive encouragement
- Post positive images and quotes around your writing space
- Find a writing coach
- Replace any of the negative thoughts that come through with positive ones. If you hear, "You can't write," replace it with, "I AM A WRITER AND THEREFORE, I WRITE!" See, that was easy.

Don't get distracted by these inner voices. Keep your mind on writing and not on critiquing yourself. This way you'll overcome these thoughts and learn to shut them down quickly.

DEVELOP A CUSTOMIZED WRITING SCHEDULE

How many words can you key in an hour or a half-hour? We'll use these factors to create a customized writing schedule. Why does this matter? Because you can discover your peak performance hours based on your word count, then schedule time to complete your book even faster than anticipated.

Before we create your schedule, let's look at the standard word count for different types of books. You'll also find this list posted in *Chapter 6—Words Count.*

- Novella — a story with 10,000 to 40,000 words
- Non-fiction — 80,000 words*
- Novel — a manuscript of 40,000 to 100,000 words
- Adult Fiction word count is 80,000 to 100,000 words
- Science Fiction and Fantasy top the word count list at 150,000 (generally they are 90,000 to 120,000 words)
- Romance novels come in at 50,000 to 100,000 words
- Historical fiction caters to contemporary audiences at 90,000 to 120,000 words
- Crime, Mysteries, Thrillers and Horror fiction readers are comfortable at 70,000 to 90,000 words
- Young Adult fiction (YA—a widely profitable genre) readers are comfortable at 50,000 to 70,000 words, although some series have longer individual titles

Kindle books (and other digital books)
- General non-fiction, 2,000 to 10,000+ words
- Fiction, short stories, 5,000 words
- Novel, 50,000 words
- Compilation of short stories, 30,000 words

Let's create a customized writing schedule for a 50,000-word book. We'll write two hours a week for four days (total of eight hours a week).

Using 800 words per hour produces 6,400 words a week. At this rate, it will take approximately 8 weeks to produce a 50,000-word book. Look at the accompanying chart to see how this computes for your writing schedule:

E-book	3 weeks	20,000 words
Small paperback	5 weeks	32,000 words
Business book	8 weeks	50,000 words

Here's another scenario. Let's say you write 500 words an hour and write eight hours a week (two hours a day for two days and four hours on weekends).

Don't be discouraged by this limited schedule. Sure, it's less aggressive than the previous one, but that's all right. You are giving this project the time you have to give, and it will pay off in the end.

At a total of 4,000 words a week you're set to produce these resources:

E-book	5 weeks	20,000 words
Small paperback	7 weeks	32,000 words
Business book	12.5 weeks	50,000 words

The following factors may influence productivity:
- Whether or not you're prepared to write
- Your writing frequency—generally, the more you write, the easier it is to get into the flow
- The longer the gap between writing sessions, the more energy you will need to get back into the flow
- You can reduce or expand your word count through editing
- Rewrites may also cause attrition or expansion
- Whether or not you can increase your writing time or your word count per session

Can you follow these simple examples? Let's try another one. As a Night Writer, you can only write six hours a week, including weekends. You can key 800 words an hour for a total of 4,800-words per week. At this rate, how long will it take you to complete your book? Check your math against ours:

E-book	5 weeks	24,000 words
Small paperback	7 weeks	33,600 words
Business book	11 weeks	52,800 words

Here's how to work this formula to calculate the word count you'll need for your writing project:

1. Determine the total word count per week (the words per hour x the number of hours a week)
2. Divide the projected word count needed for your book by your weekly word count (from above)
3. Total number of weeks projected to complete your book
4. You can, of course, knock off this time even faster by adding more hours to your schedule on the weekend or taking a writing vacation

You can take your writing to the next level by adding writing appointments to your daily/weekly/monthly calendar. Be sure to make these appointments a priority and show up. If your calendar offers color features, you can highlight your writing schedule with bright colors to make it stand out.

Having your appointments written on your schedule helps you remember them. This is accountability to yourself and the perfect way to write to the finish.

WRAPPING UP

As you can see, honing your skills is a valuable way to increase productivity. As you'll learn from *Appendix A—Productivity Tools*, there are lots of tools, tips and apps available to today's writer to support you along the writing journey.

Don't get overwhelmed by the number of tools we've listed. This book is written for writers of all genres and all levels of publishing, from debut writers to repeat writers.

Yes, even repeat writers can have their skills improved upon.

Be careful with these tools. Don't try to use everything. You may need to check out two or three resources to identify the ones that fit your more pressing need. Don't consider the examination period a waste of time. A fair evaluation is needed to determine the tool's use for your need. And remember, if it doesn't save you time, it's probably not the right tool for you.

5

Discover Your Writing Rhythm

Do you know any writers who get up at the crack of dawn to get their writing in for the day? One writer friend arises at 4:30 a.m. to get her morning started. The writing starts after her exercise and liquid breakfast. I envy these people a bit, but I don't want to be one of them. The time they're up is my time to sleep. And there's nothing wrong with either of us.

You see, I've discovered my writing rhythm, and so have they. My writing time begins at 7:30 am. This is when my thoughts run fresh and abundantly. I can write until 9:30 or 10 without any distractions. If more writing is needed for the day, I start again around 7 p.m. and write for a few more hours. This is usually when I tackle a not-so-challenging chapter.

WHAT IS WRITING RHYTHM?

In this chapter we'll delve into two types of rhythm. The first is your personal writing rhythm and the second is the rhythm of your content. Let's look at your personal writing rhythm first.

Your writing rhythm is the time of day when your energy is better for writing than at any other time. It's the time when your productive juices are flowing at their best. You are alert and excited about writing. Like other Night Writers, you attest to early morning being their best time for writing. And the second-best time is the late evening.

The same holds true for Night Writers who are full-time (day job) mothers of small children. The results from a recent social media survey on this topic favored the early morning for getting their writing done. This rang true for career mothers who work full-time out of the home. They thought it was best to complete their writing before the unexpected activities of the day ate up their scheduled writing time.

"My name is CONSISTENCY. I'm related to SUCCESS. We should hang out more often."

Anonymous

RHYTHM CREATES A MOOD

A large part of discovering your writing rhythm is acknowledging when you are joyfully productive. It's your peak time. If you feed good, you write better. You want to feel good about what you are penning and you hope it requires fewer corrections when it's time to edit.

In searching out your rhythm, you should reach what some call your "sweet spot," a mythical place where your fingers can't move fast enough. The thoughts are flowing and there's a welcomed tension between hearing it and keying it in before the thought is lost. And so it continues, like a great symphonic crescendo. The intensity drives you to create more and more content. If only you could keep this writing rhythm for the entire length of your book. You'd live happily ever after.

Much to your dismay, you've maxed out the intensity of this movement. This rhythm comes to an unwanted end. Either the alarm screams at you or your thoughts dissipate as quickly as

Oops!

Despite our best efforts, we still missed a few typos. Please ensure we (and know they) will be corrected in the next printing.

S. Hemphill

they surfaced. It's over for now so you move on with other matters in your life. Yet there's the fear that you might repeat this scenario at your next scheduled session.

Some writers miss catching their writing rhythm because they are over-focused on completing their writing assignments for the day. Their scheduled writing time has become routine; they can't resume their former writing rhythm. They may need to change something in their writing environment to increase their sensitivity to their writing rhythm.

PLANNING AND RHYTHM

If you're trying to tackle two major tasks at one time (writing a book and working a job), then your time is scarce. Therefore, you'll need to budget your time wisely. This will allow you to optimize your time on and off the job. Make use of the following tips to aid you in planning and writing your book:

- Always plan your writing session in advance
- If possible, schedule on a weekly or monthly basis
- Create either a physical calendar or a digital one
- Print out a copy of your schedule to post in your office
- Highlight your writing schedule on your digital calendar
- Honor your commitment; don't alter it unless it's a serious emergency
- See "*It's Not Your Time; It's Your Skill*" in Chapter 4 to calculate the time you need to complete your book

Ultimately, these tips will shift you closer to becoming a successful Night Writer. Adjust them to fit your particular needs. Add to them to create a customized writing platform that further enhances your writing rhythm.

MORE FACTORS TO ENHANCE YOUR WRITING RHYTHM

A writer's job is to write. This is why your writing rhythm is so important. You don't want to waste time correcting missteps in the writing process. You'll want to use your energy to cultivate the necessary attitudes to produce your best work. It may take a while to reach your sweet spot. But in due time you will discover how to start your day at peak performance

take a while to hit your sweet spot. But in due time you'll discover the set up for starting your day at peak performance.

Consider this expanded list of actions a Night Writer can use to enhance their quality of writing:

- Surround yourself with encouraging items such as framed quotes or pictures
- If you have a window nearby, try to face it. Even if you're writing when its dark, the window will represent daylight
- If you can work with fragrances, try an herbal mister or light some scented candles in your writing space
- Does music motivate you? Check out the *Reference* section for a few sites of relaxing music
- What about a special coffee or tea that you only drink to start your writing session? It smells good and it can signal something good will happen on your computer.
- As much as possible, eliminate clutter (it will distract you and stagnate your brain's peak performance). If needed, try a standing floor screen to hide an unsightly view
- Keep critical editing tools nearby (digital resources such as *Grammarly* or an online thesaurus are great aids)
- Make use of an online timer
- Purchase a comfy chair or a pad for the one you have
- Keep a high-volume thumb drive available for backing up your work

DISTRACTIONS YOU'LL WANT TO AVOID

Prepare yourself for peak performance by attending to this brief list of suggestions:

- Turn off your phone and notifications from your computer and other electronic devices

- Turn the TV off
- Avoid restricting clothing
- If background noises cannot be eliminated, mask them with soft music
- Keep bottled water nearby
- If it's not distracting to have snacks in your work space, keep dried fruit and nuts nearby (use them during a break if you use the Pomodoro Technique)

With a bit of care and preparation, you can easily optimize your writing time and enhance your writing rhythm. You'll complete your book successfully and prepare yourself to write the next one.

MINIMIZING PROCRASTINATION

It's inevitable that at one point or another, you'll fall prey to procrastination. It's a time suck that you'll want to avoid at all costs. Talk about delaying progress—it will get you every time if you don't prepare for it.

Can you totally side-step procrastination? Yes you can, but it requires preparation. Fear fuels procrastination. You can conquer these fears by using various incentives to motivate you.

If you are scared of facing a blank page, start with a chapter outline, or by asking a question about the chapter. Key in a sentence and expand on it. Or instead of fearing a deadline, create a writing calendar to keep your writing on track.

Procrastination is deciding to not write. Only you can decide how to use your time effectively. If you can decide to not write, you can decide to write.

Here is a brief list of 10 ways to beat procrastination every time it rears its ugly head. You are advised to make use of this list whenever needed. Here we go:

1. **Clarify your passion**. When you remember why you are writing, you'll be motivated to get on with the task at hand.
2. **Write from discipline**. Sometimes passion alone isn't enough. That's when habit takes over. Write because it's your time to write and your space to write.

3. **Procrastination delays your writing goals**. Some writers find it easy to put off writing. Some put it off entirely while others get stuck-in-the-middle and don't move forward. But both face the same characteristics. Only you can decide how you will use your allotted time.
4. **Shift your tasks**. If chapter one isn't provoking you, that's okay. What about shifting to another chapter to get started? Either way, keep working.
5. **Reward yourself.** You can set up your own reward system to shift your focus from not writing, to writing. For example, if you complete six hours of writing in a day, you could treat yourself to an extra day off.
6. **Flex your schedule**. Is it possible to reverse your schedule for a day or two? Instead of writing in the morning, can you write in the evening, or set up a mid-day session? Simply making a time change could be enough to get your writing juices flowing in a new and productive way.
7. **Take 5**. Really? Aren't we already having a problem getting started? Yes, but this break is deliberate instead of a stalling tactic. Leave the environment for a few minutes, then return with a fresh idea in your head.
8. **Best yourself**. Make your last writing session a benchmark you want to surpass during the next session.
9. **Chunk your writing session**. How can you reduce the demands of your writing assignment? Break it up into bite-size pieces. If you plan to write a chapter, start by listing the sub-headings. Now review the list to determine which topic catches your eye. Start here.
10. **Set up an accountability system**. You don't have to write on an island. Build an external support system to

keep you on task. Consider finding a writing buddy, joining a writing group, or asking friends to monitor your activity.

Here's some good news—your page is no longer blank. You pressed through your procrastinating mindset and have words on paper. You trumped it with your write-to-the-finish mindset. You're now on track to complete your writing journey.

THE RHYTHM OF YOUR CONTENT

The other form of rhythm mentioned before is the rhythm of your content. It reflects how the words in your content relate to each other.

Rhythm is usually related to music. Yet there is a rhythm in writing that makes your content, uh, dance. Your reader can sense the rhythm of your writing. Yes, your content can hop or skip and put a smile on the face of your reader. A pleasing rhythm keeps your reader engaged.

Content rhythm is defined as the relationship between punctuation and the stress patterns of words in a sentence. Long sentences sound smooth; short sentences can make your content sharp. If your content lacks rhythm your reader will easily become bored. If your sentence structure repeats the same structure and rhythm, your writing becomes boring.

Whether you write fiction or non-fiction, you'll want your sentences to have a continuous flow. You don't want your writing to stutter or stumble or cause a clang to the listening ear.

To check the rhythm of your content, read a chapter our loud. Look for gaps in your sentences and gaps between the paragraphs. If these sentences are harmonious, you've passed the test. This also means you have shifted from readers to fans who will want more of your future content.

WRAPPING UP

The idea of discovering your writing rhythm is to allow you to dive into a productive writing ritual. The more you write, the better the chances of your writing improving.

At this point, you have been given the keys you need to create a successful book. You know how to start writing, how to avoid procrastination, and how to complete your book with the least amount of distractions. If you apply the tips given here, your writing is bound to improve. Imagine what will happen when you apply four or five or these tips.

We encourage you to take these tips and customize them to meet your specific needs. While general in nature, they can be adjusted to create the most productive schedule possible for your particular needs. Give them a try; test them out and find the ones that work best for you.

The more tools you have in your arsenal, the better prepared you are to remove all writing hindrances. Allow me to rephrase this. The more usable tools you have in your arsenal ... you get the point. You'll avoid delays and position yourself to optimize your writing sessions. This holds true only if you have the tools you need, and you've made them serve you rather than you serving them.

Feel free to share with us any tools you find that aren't covered here. We'd love to know what else is available, and we're willing to share them with our readers.

On our website, Work Your Book (www.workyoubook.com), we keep an updated list of tools under the heading, "Sandee Recommends." We'd love to add your tips to our list. Feel free to check it out for yourself and make recommendations as you discover new resources.

6

Words Count

If you're writing a book for the first-time, one of the most difficult features of the process is that of word count. This issue holds true whether you're a Night Writer or a day shift (full-time) writer. So exactly how do you decide the best length for a book?

Let's begin by listing the word count for the most common book genres. Take note that a standard general fiction book (6 x 9) will contain 30,000 words per 100 pages (300 words per page). Publishers tend to limit general fiction to 80,000 words (between 240 and 280 pages). Here are other word counts to consider as suggested by traditional publishers:
- Novella — a story with 10,000 to 40,000 words
- Non-fiction — 80,000 words*
- Novel — a manuscript of 40,000 to 100,000 words
- Adult Fiction is 80,000 to 100,000 words
- Science Fiction and Fantasy top the word count list at 150,000 (generally they are 90,000 to 120,000 words)
- Romance novels come in at 50,000 to 100,000 words
- Historical Fiction caters to contemporary audiences at 90,000 to 120,000 words
- Crime, Mysteries, Thrillers and Horror fiction readers are comfortable at 70,000 to 90,000 words

- Young Adult Fiction (YA readers)—a widely profitable genre at 50,000 to 70,000 words, although some series have longer individual titles

The non-fiction genre fluctuates due to its various subheadings, such as memoir, history, photography, reference, and more. Therefore, 80,000 words is a baseline.

Kindle books (and other digital books)
- General Non-fiction, 2,000 to 10,000+ words
- Fiction, short stories, 5,000 words
- Novel, 50,000 words
- Compilation of Short Stories, 30,000 words

Regardless of your book genre, you'll want to compute your word count by its usefulness to the reader, and not solely on a pre-determined word count. You always want to give your readers what they want. This is how you become a successful writer.

Did you notice I didn't cover e-books in any detail? This is because it's a classification all to itself. When most people think of e-books they immediately think of Kindle. That's probably because Amazon is the world's largest bookseller. They serve as the #1 bookshelf for lots of writers. We'll cover this topic briefly due to the sheer impact of Amazon on the publishing industry.

It's difficult for some writers to even consider writing an e-book, especially as a Night Writer. However, this could be the perfect way to break into the publishing market. It all depends on your audience and your publishing goals.

You see it's quite difficult for a first-time writer to generate massive sales from their first book. Therefore, an e-book can give you the time and opportunity to build a readership and prepare them for your longer book. But that's another topic. Let's get back to the topic of *Words Count.*

WHY WORD COUNT MATTERS

Historically, first-time writers pen manuscripts that are far too long for the publishing industry. Publishers calculate the word count of a book by multiplying the page count by 250.

If you query a publisher, they'll want only 5-10 pages of the book for-warded to them. They request the total word count be included in the query letter.

Over-the-limit word count is one of the key reasons for reject-ion of first submissions. The higher the word count (usually over 90,000 words for a novel), the less chance it will sell.

When it comes to lengthy word count, here are some except-ions to the rules:

Harry Potter Series
The Philosopher's Stone — 76,944 words
The Chamber of Secrets — 85,141 words
The Prisoner of Azkaban — 107,253 words
The Goblet of Fire — 190,637 words
The Order of the Phoenix — 257,045 words
The Half-Blood Prince — 168,923 words
The Deathly Hallows — Approximately 198,227 words

Lord Of The Rings
The Hobbit — 95,022 words
Fellowship of the Ring — 177,227 words
Two Towers — 143,436 words
Return of the King — 134,462 words

Twilight Series
Twilight — 118,501 words *(this is unusually long for a first-time novel)*
New Moon — 132,807 words
Eclipse — 147,930 words
Breaking Dawn — 192,196 words

The Hunger Games — 99,750 words

A Game of Thrones — 298,000 words

A Clash of Kings — 326,000 words

A Dance with Dragons — 422,000

You can choose to break this writing rule, and lots of writers do. However, if I were a first-time writer, I'd work hard to stay within the acceptable norm.

Here's a word count tidbit you may not know. *The Sound and the Fury,* William Faulkner's epic story, includes a 600-word section with no punctuation

---

"The best way to get something done is to begin."

— Anonymous

WORD COUNT AND READER ENGAGEMENT

According to Michael Hyatt, author and former chairman and CEO of Thomas Nelson Publishing, reports that readers' bail out on finishing (reading) books they register as "too long." Consider these numbers:
- At 100 pages or less, 60% of readers will finish the book
- At 200 pages, only 20% will finish the book
- If your book is more than 200 pages, a mere 3% will finish

Reader engagement should be paramount in your present and future writing projects. Keep this information in mind as you prepare your manuscript for publication. I'm certain there are exceptions to this list. However, by giving these statistics consideration, you'll keep your writing marketable and readable to the last page.

WRAPPING UP

Did you realize how important this topic is? Word count plays an important role in writing because word count helps you tailor your book to your ideal readers. Note the comments about when readers bail out of reading a book based upon word count.

Use this information to your advantage and make sure your book fits your readers' interest. A reader of novels will balk at a thin book sitting on a store's bookshelf. And a self-help reader will pass on a book that looks like War and Peace.

As you can see, there is a definite place for word count and how your potential readers might respond to your book. If you stay within these guidelines, you should be able to write books that sell, and sell well.

Of course, you can ignore all of the information presented here and draft the book you *think* your readers will like. This is often what debut writers do; they write the book they want, not the book their readers need. However, if you ignore this information, you'll do so at your own peril.

The statistics presented here are a guideline to keep you on target with what sells. After all, you're not writing a book to give it away, are you? Of course, not. You're writing a book to sell and one that will cause your readers to gravitate towards you and your other books, and related products and services.

The idea of word count is to know your readers and cater to their specific reading needs. Then you'll find readers' who will enjoy your books, readers who are loyal to you, and readers who will excitedly await your next book.

If you can accomplish this reader goal, you'll easily evolve into the successful writer you hoped to become.

7

Crossing the Finish Line

Have you ever won an award or accomplished something that was challenging in your life? If so, then you understand the rush of pride and self-worth you experience when you realize what you've done.

It's an incredible feeling. The rush of adrenaline tells you the task at hand has come to a successful end. And this doesn't only happen the first time you reach your goal; you can have this experience each time you cross the finish line of any writing project.

"This one makes a net, this one stands and wishes.
Would you like to make a bet which one gets the fishes?"
Chinese Rhyme

Think about it. You summoned your drive and determination to push you through a challenge and bring you to the end. You've accomplished a new goal and now know that you are capable of anything. New challenges face you and you're ready to go at it once again.

If you haven't had this feeling lately, you can experience it now as you cross the finish line of this book. You've made it to the end and will be a better writer for your efforts.

Let's take a quick review of what we've discussed:
- What's a Night Writer?
- Debunking Negative Self-Talk and Writing/Working Myths
- Plan or Plunge: The Outline Dilemma
- It's Not Your Time, Its Your Skill
- Discover Your Writing Rhythm
- Words Count
- Crossing the Finish Line

This book is designed to be a short read in an effort to provide a quick and easy resource for Night Writers. After all, Night Writers are pressed for time as it is. And your priority for now is writing and not necessarily reading. It's possible for this book to be longer. However, if it accomplishes its true goal, the extra length would be of no benefit.

Instead, we've loaded the book with fresh insights, tips and resources for Night Writers at all stages of development. After reading it, you'll be more equipped for publishing success than writers who don't purchase a copy.

And that's not all ... there's more to come.

Check out the Appendices to find lots of added information to guide you through your publishing journey. It's one of the key features of this book, with a list of more than 60 resources to help you upgrade your skills and write better and faster.

All told, you'll soon be equipped to draft a best seller and receive the literary accolades you long for. These can either be local, national or international acknowledgements that eluded you. They're now in reach and you're qualified to grab them.

Allow me to be the first to congratulate you on a job well done and to wish you continued publishing success.

"

THIS IS HOW YOU DO IT.
YOU SIT DOWN AT THE KEYBOARD
AND YOU PUT ONE WORD AFTER
ANOTHER UNTIL IT'S DONE.

**IT'S THAT EASY,
AND THAT HARD."**

— Neil Gaiman —

Here's an idea I've found to be extremely effective in helping me stay focused on my writing tasks.

I make prints of the book's cover and place them in my writing environment. If I'm in my office it's on the corkboard near the desk—always visible.

If I go out to work remotely (library, eatery, etc.), I bring a smaller copy to place on the desk or tabletop. This gives me instant focus on the finished product and helps me stay motivated.

A writer colleague of mine puts her cover on her device's home screens to remind her that writing is a priority. As she nears the end of her project, she adds wording such as "Best-Seller" or "James Patterson Award" to her graphic.

When it comes to writing, every bit of inspiration and encouragement helps. Whatever it takes to keep you motivated, do it.

Happy Publishing!

Appendix A

30 Productivity Tools To Get You
To The Finish Line — Faster Than Expected

Hemingway
Does the excessive use of adverbs and long sentences clog up your writing? Not sure of how to use the passive voice? If this is you, then this grammar editor meets your need. It covers these common writing pitfalls and much more.
Get it here: www.hemingwayapp.com

Phraseology
This is a tablet user's dream come true. It offers an extended keyboard and iCloud storage access. If you write away from home, take this one with you. Sorry, this one is Apple only.
Get it here: http://agiletortoise.com/phraseology

Coach.me
Here's a multi-platform app designed to help you build new habits. It's a motivator and word count tracker all in one.
Get it here: http://www.coach.me

Pomodoro Technique
We discussed this in some detail in Chapter 4. Here's a link for additional information.
Get it here: http://graemeshimmin.com/the-pomodoro-technique-for-writers

The Brainstormer
Need a fresh plotline twist? This app stimulates a plotline by spinning three separate wheels that provide you with the conflict, the setting and the subject of the story. It offers an endless array of plot options.
Get it here: http://www.tapnik.com/brainstormer

Creative Writer
This app offers words, sentences and suggestions from some historical texts. It offers a dictionary and a functional notepad. Available at the App Store.
Get it here: http://resonanca-it.com/creative-writer

Mindnode
This app lets you brainstorm and map out your ideas. You can add photos and notes. This app is visually stunning and practical at the same time. Available for Apple only. *Get it here: https://mindnode.com/*

Mindly
This is a free app available on iPhone or Android that allows you to map out your idea for a script, article or even a speech. You can take notes, attach images and export to other formats.
Get it here: http://www.mindlyapp.com

Storylist
Get the mobile functionality you need with this app. You can organize what you've written and display it in a clean format to enhance the creative process.
Get it here: http://storyist.com/

Story Tracker
Get organized; track submissions to editors or publications; take notes. These are the prominent features of this app. It's like having a virtual assistant in your pocket!
Get it here:
http://andrewnicolle.com/all_apps/storytracker (iOS)
http://andrewnicolle.com/all_apps/story-tracker-for-mac (Mac)
http://andrewnicolle.com/all_apps/story-tracker-for-pc (PC)

Trello
Trello is a web-based productivity tool. It mimics index cards on a corkboard and offers endless writer possibilities. Use it for to-do lists, research, prioritize submissions, and more.
Get it here: https://trello.com

FocusOn
Here's an easy way to block distractions, but be careful. Once you turn it on it's hard to cancel a block that you've set up. *Available at Apple Store, iTunes and Google Play.*

TimeWarp, Self Control, StayFocused, FocusLock
Do you give in to B.S.O.'s (bright shiny objects)? Try these:
+ TimeWarp (Chrome) — *http://bit.ly/ChromeStore2017*
+ Self Control (Mac) — *https://selfcontrolapp.com*
+ StayFocused (Chrome) — *http://bit.ly/ChromeStore2017*
+ FocusLock (Android) — *https://play.google.com/store*

Brain Wave
This unique app plays music to set the mood for productive writing. It also provides binaural frequencies designed to stimulate the brain towards either motivation or productivity.
Available at the App Store.

Omniwriter
A desktop or mobile app to help writers focus by removing internet-related distractions. It keeps you focused on writing.
Get it here: www.omniwriter.com

Novel in 30
This app lets you turn your device into a distraction-free writing environment. It offers an enhanced keyboard with the ability to set milestones and track your progress.
Get it here: http://www.novelin30.com/tour.html

Evernote
This is a masterful productivity app that takes notes and organize your digital space to recording full-screen shoots. Available free everywhere. *Get it here: https://evernote.com*

Zotero
A Firefox extension that let's you capture bibliographic info from web pages, organize citations and create bibliographies.
Get it here: https://www.zotero.org

Appendix A

Scrivener
Designed specifically for creative writers; it offers full control over the word processor for editing your writing projects.
Get it here: https://www.literatureandlatte.com/trial.php

Write or Die
Configure your writing period, word goal, and the punishment should your fingers stop typing. Now type continuously.
Get it here: http://writeordie.com

Notability
Available on the Apple platform, this app turns your device into the perfect note-taking tool. You can make sketches, mark photos and PDFs, and other useful tasks.
Get it here: http://gingerlabs.com

After the Deadline
This is a powerful spell checker for catching common writing errors and misused words. It uses Artificial Intelligence to recommend smart alternatives. It houses 1,500 misused words and suggests words for better writing.
Get it here: http://www.afterthedeadline.com

AutoCrit
The Autocrit app is made specifically for fiction writers. The main focus is in areas of pacing, dialogue, momentum, word choice, repetition and strong writing.
Get it here: https://www.autocrit.com

Grammarly
This free online grammar checker searches out and destroys hundreds of grammar and spelling mistakes.
Get it here: https://www.grammarly.com

SmartEdit
A downloadable editing tool (Windows only) with 20 different types of checks on your content plus clichés and redundancies.
Get it here: http://www.smart-edit.com

MultiMarkdown
This is a tool to help turn minimally mark-up plain text into well-formatted documents (HTML, PDF or OpenDocument). You write without style or spacing concerns.
Get it here: http://multimarkdown.com

Writing Prompts and Character Prompts
A variety of sites offer writing prompts and character prompts with profile characteristics, thousands of character twists, and character questions to help you develop your storyline.
Get it here: http:// yeahwrite.co/prompts

Writer's Block Buster
An application for writers of all genres: fiction, nonfiction, technical and more; consistently sparks creative fires.
Available at the Apple store

WordBook
A dictionary and thesaurus with etymological information, a built-in spell checker with pop-up suggestions.
Available at the Apple and Android stores

Mind Mapping Apps and Programs
Here is a list of mind mapping tools to assist writers of all genres. Try out several to find the one that works for you.

- Mindmeister — *https://www.mindmeister.com*
- Imindmap — *Apple and Android stores*
- Spiderscribe — *https://www.spiderscribe.net*
- Xmind — *http://www.xmind.net*
- Freemind — *Apple and Android stores*
- Text2mindmap — *Available at the Apple store*

Use this link [http://bit.ly/NightWriterLinks]
to download the links from this section.
No e-mail address is required.

Appendix B:
Q&A from LinkedIn Group

This question was asked of one of my LinkedIn groups. The answers are given here by permission of the writers.

Question

> *"Are you writing while working 9 to 5 (or any 8-hour shift)? Can you share how you fit writing into your life?"*

Answers

I write when I feel like it. You can't force writing, because it doesn't work. So I write when the creativity wants to, which is usually at the weekends, or late at night.
A.J. Humpage, author of Blood of the Father

———————————

I try and write in the evenings and during the weekend but if I find the story lines starts flowing, I have been known to write all night. I am on my second novel and even when I am out and about I am always jotting down ideas and notes for the evening.
John Needham, author of The Exploits of an 18th Century Entrepreneur - A Smugglers Tale'

———————————

[I write] 2 hours a day, 6-8 pm. even if it isn't good writing ... just write. If you stick to a specific time, it seems the muses get used to showing up at that time, and you begin to start writing well.
Ruth Gilbo, author of The Perennial Garden

———————————

Jotting down ideas, pieces of dialogue, new character's names on Post-Its and stuffing them into my accordion folder until I'm ready to really sit and write.

I am very lucky in that I don't have to wait long for timing and inspiration to collide.
Debbie Burke, **book-in-progress:**
Glissando: A Story of Love, Lust and Jazz

I am self-employed and as a result can go for weeks on my regular job without writing or even thinking of writing at all. On the other hand, when I write, it's usually at least a week at a time, and anywhere from a 6 to an 11-hour day. I like this routine because when I'm in it, I wake up with writing on my mind... problems solved or the hint of a new direction that I didn't know was there. This on-again, off-again routine does not seem to be common.... but it works for me.
Robert M. Kelly, author of The Backstory of Wallpaper

*Source: The Writer's Network, LinkedIn Group
with 29,000+ members.
https://www.linkedin.com/groups/2033716/203
3716-6228761423334432768
Printed by permission of the commenters.*

References

Books

From the Outline to the Finish Line — FREE E-book from author Shelley Hitz
http://bit.ly/ShelleyHitz

Writer's Doubt: The #1 Enemy of Writing (and What You Can Do About It — Kindle Edition) — Bryan Hutchinson

The 15-Minute Writer: How To Write Your Book In Only 15 Minutes A Day (Kindle Edition) — Jennifer Blanchard

Stop Worrying; Start Writing: How to Overcome Fear, Self-Doubt and Procrastination — Sarah Painter

Outline Your Book Step By Step (2016): 7 Easy Steps to Outlining Your Non-Fiction Book in 90 Minutes or Less — Andy Grammer

Articles

How to Create a Plot Outline in 8 Easy Steps
www.how-to-write-a-book-now.com/plot-outline.html

MultiMarkdown (presented by Michael Hyatt)
https://michaelhyatt.com/multimarkdown.html

The Pomodoro Technique
http://graemeshimmin.com/the-pomodoro-technique-for-writers

50 Creative Writing Prompts to Enrich Your Craft
http://www.nownovel.com/blog/50-creative-writing-prompts/

References

How to Self-Edit: 15 Steps from First Draft to Publication
http://www.helpingwritersbecomeauthors.com/how-i-self-edit-my-novels-15-steps-from

The Snowflake Method for Designing a Novel
http://www.advancedfictionwriting.com/articles/snowflake-method

How to Write a Story Without an Outline
http://thewritepractice.com/no-outline

Book Outline: 11 Ways to Outline a Book
http://self-publishingschool.com/11-ways-outline-book

15 Editorial Tools to Help You Outline, Write and Edit (Better and Faster)
https://zapier.com/blog/writing-editing-apps

7 Steps to Creating a Flexible Outline for Any Story
http://www.writersdigest.com/online-editor/7-steps-to-creating-a-flexible-outline-for-any-story

Websites

Time to Write — Offers tips and advice on writing, promotion and creativity.
http://www.timetowrite.blogs.com

Write Now is Good — Author and editor Kristin Gorski writes about writing, creativity, and inspiration.
http://writenowisgood.typepad.com

Write to Done — The secrets of publishing success is shared here.
http://writetodone.com

Writing Power — Real down-in-the-trenches advice on issues like narration, revision, and word usage.
http://www.writingpower.net

Writing.com — Focused around a forum where writers offer each other support, advice, online portfolio and critiques.
https://www.writing.com/?i=1

Templates (from selfpublishingteam.com)

Basic Plot Outline
http://selfpublishingteam.com/wp- content/uploads/ 2012/03/Basic-Outline.pdf

Detailed Plot Outline
http://selfpublishingteam.com/wp- content/uploads/2012/03/Detailed-Plot-Outlines.pdf

Basic Character Outline
http://selfpublishingteam.com/wp- content/uploads/2012/03/Basic-Character-Profiles.pdf

Music

Concentration Music For Studying: Music for Inspiration, Creativity and Writing, Thinking Music
https://www.youtube.com/watch?v=cH7RJEM4EYI

6 Hours of The Best Epic Inspirational Music for Studying/Working
https://youtu.be/5N8sUccRiTA

World's Most Breathtaking Piano Pieces | Contemporary Music Mix | Vol. 1
https://youtu.be/OGMJ2b-3eCk

References

YouTube Videos

5 Tips to Develop Your Fiction Writing Voice
https://youtu.be/lkFaiXrqTuQ

How to Outline Your Novel — The Storyboard
https://youtu.be/V3XmqvUmVn0

How to Improve Your Writing Skills: 7 tips to be even more productive during your writing time!
https://youtu.be/SHuNK9iBtDI

How to outline and create a framework for a non-fiction book
https://youtu.be/nd-sDUFZCc0

How to Outline a Book With Mind Mapping Software — FreeMind Tutorial
https://youtu.be/uTuqul75lUc

Outlining With Scrivener!
https://youtu.be/oryXJ18eUp8

Amazing eBook Outlines
https://youtu.be/PZtrdo81gDI

Use this link [http://bit.ly/NightWriterLinks]
to download the links from this section.
No e-mail address is required.

About the Author

"Writing has to be a passion; otherwise, it's another chore," says author Sandee Hemphill. The Atlanta native uses this sentiment in writing. It carries over to her positions as author, speaker and book-marketing strategist.

Sandee has been writing and publishing for seven years. Her books for authors cover topics from writing to launching an author platform to building your reader tribe. In addition, she writes in the Christian genre, having penned two books and has a third on the drawing board.

As a book marketer, Sandee is a crusader for first-time authors as well as veteran authors. She knows first-hand what it takes to write and publish. Therefore, she is sensitive to the many demands of book marketing.

When she's not on the keyboard, Sandee spends her time on jigsaw puzzles and enjoying British mysteries (books, audiobooks and movies,). She also enjoys walking and weight lifting, especially the kettle bell.

Sandee has penned five books for authors and two Christian books. Her next book for authors is **Build Your Tribe Before You Publish.** It is scheduled for released later this year (2017). You'll find her book list on page 84.

We Love Reviews

Now That You've Read the Book ...

... we can use your help! The publishing world is driven by sales. And sales are driven by reviews.

If you enjoyed this book, would you consider writing a review? Simply follow the instructions below. Not only will you do us a huge favor, you'll help fellow book browsers who land on the book page see the value in purchasing this book.

<u>Here's How to Write a Review on Amazon:</u>

1) Go to http://bit.ly/AuthorCentralSLH. Select this book and look for the reviews or the review link under Sandee's name. Amazon will ask you to give the book a star rating. Once you click on the stars, a window opens so you can add your written review. Please wait 2-4 days after purchase to write a review.

2) Write your review. Simply tell the readers what you think about the book (good, not so good or otherwise). Your honest opinion will do much to spread the word about this book.

3) Please include the title of the book in the review. This adds even more credit from the search engine standpoint. If you purchase the digital format, be sure to read through every page (Amazon checks to see how much you've actually read).

4) If you're a published author, I invite you to leave your book title along with your name. This creates an opportunity for you to get noticed as well.

Here's an advance "Thank You" for your review.

Reviews on Other Sites

Most online book sites will offer a review option.

In most cases, you can use the previous steps (2-4) to submit a review to those sites. You may have to search for it.

Begin by looking for stars or a review link.

If the site has requirements for the review, please adhere to them.

Feel free to read through any reviews that have been written. This may help you formulate ideas for your review.

As always, thank you in advance for leaving a review. Future readers will benefit from your insight.

Other Books by Sandee

Visit Sandee's Amazon Author Central*
Webpage to Discover Her Other Books

Publishing & Book Marketing

Publish Your First Book Now

Jumpstart Your Author Platform

Your Book Won't Sell Itself

Boost Your Holiday Book Sales

––––––––––

Christian Themed Titles

Seeking Through Soaking

Divine Appointments

*You'll find all of Sandee's books at this link:
http://bit.ly/AuthorCentralSLH

You can contact Sandee at
sandee@workyourbook.com

Get This Book... FREE!

Yes, You Can Get a Copy of the e-Book —

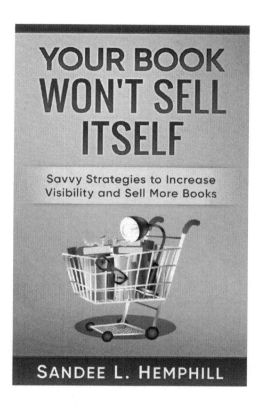

Available for immediate download when you
subscribe to our blog, WRITE BRAIN.

Use this link to get your instant download!
https://www.bit.ly/GETEBOOK

YES, SEND ME MY COPY NOW!